To ....

From ....

First published by Parragon in 2009

Parragon
Queen Street House
4 Queen Street
Bath BA1 1HE, UK

ISBN 978-1-4075-6598-9

Printed in China

First Bible
Stories for Boys

Illustrated by
Andrew Geeson and Sophie Keen

Bath · New York · Singapore · Hong Kong · Cologne · Delhi · Melbourne

The Old Testament

The New Testament

In the Very Beginning

I n the very beginning, there was nothing at all. There was nothing to see, nothing but darkness. But God was there.

God placed a warm sun to shine by day…

and a silvery moon to shine by night—and so the world began.

11

The Garden of Eden

G od filled the world with fish, birds, and animals. Last of all, God created the first man and woman, Adam and Eve. They lived in the Garden of Eden, where things were good.

In the Garden of Eden lived a cunning snake. He tricked Eve into eating an apple that God had forbidden to her. From then on, things started to go wrong.

13

Noah's Ark

Years passed, and God was unhappy at what he saw. God decided to send a huge flood to wash away everything that was bad and start again.

But Noah and his family were kind and God wanted to save them. God told Noah to build an ark and to fill it with two of every kind of animal in the world.

15

The Story
of Abraham

A braham and his wife, Sarah, were good people. They were old and although they dearly wanted children, they had none.

God promised Abraham that he would be the father of a great nation and would have a son, if he left his homeland and trusted in God. God's promise came true, and Abraham and Sarah had a son, Isaac.

Isaac and Rebecca

Abraham wanted Isaac to marry someone from his homeland. He sent his servant off on the long journey with ten camels. The tired servant arrived at a place with a well.

"Please, God, if the girl brings water for me, and the camels, she will be the right wife for Isaac," the servant prayed.

A girl called Rebecca fetched water for the servant and for the camels. This was a sign from God. She traveled back and married Isaac.

Esau and Jacob

Isaac and Rebecca had twin boys, Esau and Jacob. Isaac was old and blind. He wanted to bless Esau before he died. But Rebecca tricked him into blessing Jacob.

Esau was furious, so Rebecca sent Jacob away. Jacob had a dream. God said, "I will give you and your children the land on which you lie. I will look after you wherever you go."

Jacob trusted God. He married and had children. Esau also forgave him. Jacob's family became the children of Israel.

Joseph's Special Coat

Jacob had twelve sons, but Joseph was his favorite. Jacob gave Joseph a special coat. Joseph had dreams that were sent by God. The brothers were jealous and wanted to get rid of Joseph, so they sold him as a slave in Egypt and told Jacob he had died.

But Joseph became a trusted servant to Pharaoh. Years later, he saved Egypt from a famine and found his brothers had changed and were good. So they all lived together again, with Jacob.

23

The Story of Moses

A new Pharaoh ruled Egypt. He saw that the Israelites were powerful and was scared. He ordered that every boy born to an Israelite must be drowned. The Pharaoh's daughter found a baby boy in the river Nile. She named him Moses.

Moses grew up and was angry at how his people were being treated by the Egyptians. He heard God's voice from a burning bush, ordering Moses to find his brother, Aaron, and save the Israelites.

Free My People!

Moses and Aaron told Pharaoh that God wanted his people released from slavery. But Pharaoh didn't believe in God. "I will force Pharaoh to free my people," said God. So God made ten disasters hit Egypt.

Finally, Pharaoh set them free but then sent his soldiers after them. The Israelites were trapped, but Moses stretched out his arms and God sent a wind to blow back the water of the Red Sea. The Israelites were saved.

God's Laws

Moses and the Israelites set up camp. God told them he had brought them there to be his chosen people.

"Will you obey me?" he asked them. They agreed to obey God. God gave them ten special laws, God's laws—his "commandments."

Moses was God's special prophet and explained the laws to the people.

"Honor
and serve me alone,
for I am the only God.

Do not make or
worship any idols.

Treat my name
with respect.

Keep every Sabbath
as a day of rest.

Respect your father
and mother.

Do not
kill another
human being.

Husbands and wives
must keep their love
only for each other.

Do not steal.

Do not tell lies.

Do not be greedy
about things that
other people have."

The Walls of Jericho

When Moses died, God chose Joshua to be the new leader. This worried Joshua but God said he would be with him.

Joshua sent two spies to Jericho. The city had walls all around it. How could they capture the city? But God told Joshua what to do. The Israelites did as God said and the walls came crashing down. The Israelites slowly conquered the "promised land" with Joshua as their leader.

Strong Samson

A long time passed and the Israelites forgot about God. To punish them, God allowed the Philistines to rule over them for forty years.

A man and wife who longed for a child were visited by an angel. The angel said they would have a son, who would help protect the Israelites.

Samson was so strong that he even killed a lion with his bare hands! He used his strength to fight against the Philistines.

Naomi and Ruth

Many years passed and Israel suffered a terrible famine. Naomi's husband and sons had died, so Naomi returned to her homeland with Ruth, her son's widow.

The women were very poor. By chance, Ruth worked in the field of a rich man called Boaz. He was a relative of Naomi's. Boaz and Ruth married and had a son.

Ruth was to become the great-grandmother of Israel's greatest king—David.

Hannah's Special Son

Hannah was an Israelite. She prayed to God for a child.

Later, Hannah had a son called Samuel. God chose him to lead the Israelites. But the Israelites wanted a king, so Samuel went to find one. He found Saul, but Saul became too proud and God sent him to find a new king.

Samuel kept looking and finally found David, a young shepherd. "This is the chosen one!" said God.

David and Goliath

David continued to look after his father's sheep. He was skilful with a slingshot and played the harp.

One day, news came that the Philistines were near. A giant man, named Goliath, shouted "Where's the champion of Israel? If he kills me, we will be your slaves."

David went to fight Goliath. When Goliath saw David, he laughed. But David took aim with his slingshot. The stone struck Goliath's head and killed him. The Israelites had won!

David, King of Israel

King David made Jerusalem God's city. David was a great leader and faithful to God, but he fell in love with Bathsheba, a married woman, and had her husband killed.

David was truly sorry and God forgave him. David's son, Solomon, had the task of building God's temple. David married Bathsheba and although his kingdom was strong, his other sons attempted to take his place. But David fought against them and said Solomon would succeed him.

The Wise King Solomon

Before he died, King David told Solomon to be a strong king, to trust God and follow his commandments. "Then God will keep his promise that my descendants will rule this nation," he said.

Solomon loved God dearly. He had a dream and asked God for wisdom to help him make the right and true decisions. God was pleased with this. Solomon grew to be a great king but never forgot that his wisdom came from God.

43

The Holy Temple

Solomon built a temple for God. It took seven years to build. It was decorated with carved figures, palm trees, and flowers, all covered in gold.

Solomon decided to hold a special ceremony. "Lord, God of Israel, hear the prayers of your people. Listen to them in your home in heaven and help them always." Then Solomon turned to his people. "You must be true to God. You must obey his commandments."

Solomon Breaks His Promise

Israel prospered during Solomon's reign. He built many beautiful palaces. But Solomon spent a lot of money and his people paid heavier taxes to cover his debt.

Solomon also married many foreign princesses and built temples to worship their gods. This made God sad.

God spoke to Solomon. "The kingdom of Israel will be taken from your son, since you have not followed my commandments." And as time passed, God's words came true.

Elijah's Battle

Solomon died and Israel divided. None of the kings were faithful to God. One king and his wife worshipped her god, Baal. The queen had killed many of God's prophets, but not Elijah.

Elijah told them that there would be no rain until God said so. They were angry at Elijah, so he ran away. God sent ravens with food and protected him for three years.

Elijah returned and challenged them to prove their god, but they failed. The people cried, "The Lord is the only God."

Isaiah's Promise

A hundred years after Elijah died, life became difficult for God's people, and the land of Israel divided again. God sent the prophet Isaiah to help King Hezekiah save Jerusalem. Isaiah gave the people of Jerusalem a promise.

"Unto us a child is born, unto us a son is given. He will be called the Mighty God, Everlasting Father, Prince of Peace. There will be no end to his rule and peace."

51

Daniel and the Lions

The people continued to disobey God, so he let the king of Babylon gain control of Jerusalem. People were taken prisoner, including a young man called Daniel. Daniel and some friends were chosen to serve the royal court.

Babylon was then captured by the Persians. Daniel became a chief advisor, and the other advisors became jealous. They tricked Daniel and had him thrown to the lions. But God kept Daniel safe. Everyone knew then that God was the one true God.

Jonah and the Whale

God wanted Jonah to deliver a message, but Jonah disobeyed. God was angry, so he sent a storm when Jonah was at sea. Jonah knew it was his fault so asked the captain to throw him overboard.

As Jonah sank he called out. God heard him and sent a whale to swallow him up alive. Jonah stayed inside for three whole days. He prayed to God. God listened and forgave him, and so the whale let him out. Jonah then delivered God's message.

God's Promise

O ver the years, there were many times when God's people forgot to obey his laws. His prophets warned what would happen if people didn't change their ways.

But one prophet, Micah, told people about God's special promise. He told them that God was going to send a ruler for Israel. This special ruler would come from the town of Bethlehem.

The prophet was telling people about Jesus. Jesus' story is told in the New Testament.

The New Testament

Jesus Is Born

The Angel Gabriel visited Mary and said, "You are going to have a special baby, God's own son. You will call the baby Jesus."

Mary was engaged to Joseph. The angel visited Joseph in his dreams and told him about God's plans.

They traveled to Bethlehem. All the inns were full, so they stayed in a stable, and that is where Jesus was born.

A Star in the East

T hree wise men noticed a star shining more brightly than all the others. They knew this meant that a great king had been born.

They followed the star and traveled for many days and nights, finally arriving in Bethlehem.

They saw the baby Jesus with his mother, Mary. They gave Jesus gifts of gold, frankincense, and myrrh.

Jesus Is Baptized

God had chosen John to be his messenger. People came from far and wide to hear him preach. "God's king is coming soon," he said. "Be baptized, and God will forgive you for the things that you have done wrong."

One day Jesus arrived. John knew at once that Jesus was God's promised king. So John baptized him. As Jesus came up out of the water, a dove landed on his shoulder and God's voice said, "This is my own blessed son."

The Wedding Wine

John was thrown into prison, so Jesus continued preaching John's message.

One day Jesus was invited to a wedding. Halfway through the celebrations the wine ran out. Jesus asked for some water jugs to be filled with water. When the man in charge took a sip, the water had changed into the most delicious wine.

This was Jesus' first miracle.

Follow Me!

Soon many people had heard about Jesus, and as he walked, Jesus met people who were to become his followers.

In all, Jesus chose twelve of his most loyal followers to be his special friends, or "disciples."

Jesus explained why God had sent him to Earth. His disciples traveled with him wherever he went, and saw all the amazing things he did.

Be Still!

Jesus and his followers set off in a boat. Soon the gentle lapping of the water had lulled Jesus to sleep.

Suddenly the wind changed and the calm water turned to huge waves. The storm got worse. But still Jesus slept. "Master, wake up!" his followers shouted.

Jesus awoke. "Be still!" he said. The storm stopped immediately.

"Where is your faith?" asked Jesus. All they could do was stare in awe and wonder.

Jesus Cures the Sick

People talked about Jesus curing the sick. Crowds came from all over the land just to be touched by him.

A man went to see Jesus. "Please help me. My only daughter is dying." Jesus followed the man, but so many people stopped him that the girl died before he reached her.

The man was heartbroken but Jesus said, "Trust me. The girl is just sleeping." Jesus held out his hand. At once, the little girl sat up and opened her eyes.

Five Loaves and Two Fishes

One day Jesus was teaching by Lake Galilee. By sunset, five thousand people were still gathered around him. They were all hungry!

A little boy offered Jesus five barley loaves and two fishes. Jesus took the food and thanked God. Then he gave the food to his disciples, who broke it up and handed it out to the people.

Everyone ate as much as they needed, and there were twelve baskets of food left over!

A Good Friend

The religious leaders became jealous of Jesus. They tried to trick him with difficult questions. "Who is my neighbor?" one asked. Jesus told a story.

"One day a man was walking when he was beaten up and left for dead. A priest and a teacher didn't stop to help him. Finally a Samaritan stopped, cleaned his wounds, and took him to an inn."

"The Samaritan was a good friend," said the teacher.

"Then try to be like him," said Jesus.

The Story of Lazarus

F riends of Jesus sent him a message to say that their brother, Lazarus, was very ill. Two days later, Jesus and his disciples went to his friend. But Lazarus had already died.

"Take me to Lazarus's grave," said Jesus. Then he called out, "Lazarus! Come out!" Instantly Lazarus walked out of the tomb.

Many people believed that God had sent Jesus, but others did not. "Soon everyone will follow this man," they muttered. And Jesus' enemies began to plot his death.

The Plot Against Jesus

The disciples were getting ready for the Passover festival. But Judas no longer believed that Jesus was the son of God. He went to talk to the priests.

"How much will you pay me to betray him?" Judas asked the priests.

One of the priests pulled out a bag of money. "Tell us where we will find Jesus as soon as you can," he said. From that moment, Judas watched Jesus, waiting for the right moment to betray him.

81

The Last Supper

Jesus knew that his enemies were searching for him. Jesus and his disciples sat down to eat the Passover meal. "One of you is going to betray me," said Jesus. The disciples were upset.

No one saw Judas leave the room. When he had gone Jesus said, "Do not be afraid. God's spirit will always be with you."

Jesus knew this would be his last meal with his friends.

Jesus' Friends Leave Him

When the meal was finished, Jesus and his disciples went to a peaceful garden to pray. "Tonight you will all leave me," he said. This upset his disciples.

Jesus heard voices and knew it was the soldiers coming to arrest him. Leading them was Judas. The guards surrounded Jesus. Jesus' disciples watched in dismay and, just as he had predicted, they ran away and left him!

Jesus Is Put To Death

The Jewish priests said that Jesus claimed to be the son of God, which was against their law. They brought him to the Roman court, where he was sentenced to death.

Roman soldiers whipped Jesus and made him wear a crown of thorns. Like all prisoners about to be crucified, Jesus had to carry a huge wooden cross. Jesus felt pity for the soldiers. "Father, forgive them," he prayed to God.

At three o'clock, Jesus died. His suffering was over at last.

The Empty Tomb

Two men who were followers of Jesus prepared his body for burial. They carried him to a tomb and rolled a large stone across the front of the cave.

On Sunday Mary Magdalene and some friends went to the tomb. The entrance was open! They saw an angel sitting where Jesus' body had been. "He is risen from the dead. Go and tell his disciples the good news," the angel said.

They ran off, leaving Mary behind. Mary saw a stranger and knew it was Jesus!

Jesus Returns!

Later that Sunday two friends were walking home, talking about Jesus. A stranger joined them and asked why they were sad. He told them that it was God's plan that Jesus would die, but would live again. Then he vanished.

As the men told their story, Jesus appeared. The disciples were frightened. "Is it a ghost?" they said. But Jesus showed them the nail marks on his hands and feet. His followers knew that Jesus had risen from the dead.

The Holy Spirit

Jesus knew it was time for him to go home to heaven. He spoke with his disciples. "Teach other people about me," he said. "God will send you his holy spirit." Then he was gone.

In Jerusalem, Jesus' disciples were touched by flames. They were filled with the Holy Spirit, and suddenly they could speak in different languages. Now they could spread the news about Jesus to everyone.

People continue to gather together to hear God's message.

93